Changing Forms of

by Colin Kong

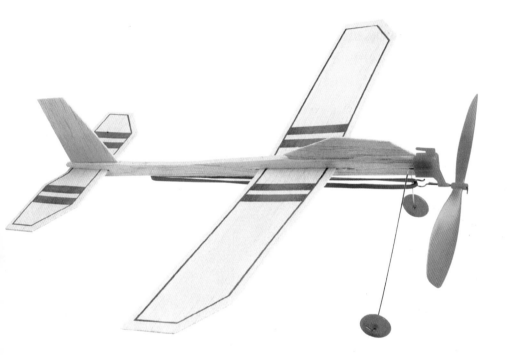

PEARSON
Scott
Foresman

DK

What is energy?

Forms of Energy

In science, energy has a very specific meaning. **Energy** is the ability to do work or cause a change. It can change an object's qualities such as motion, color, shape, or temperature.

Energy has many forms, and it is all around you. Some forms you know about are sound, light, electricity, and magnetism. Bonds holding molecules together have chemical energy. Nuclear energy holds the nucleus of an atom together. Mechanical energy is the energy of movement. When an object becomes warmer, it usually gains thermal energy.

Fireworks can change chemical energy to thermal, light, and sound energy.

Energy cannot be made or destroyed. But it can move from one object to another. Energy can also change form. Fireworks have chemical energy. When the fireworks are lit, hot gases form as chemical energy changes to thermal energy. Then the fireworks explode, producing light and sound energy.

Many devices we use can change energy. A light bulb changes electrical energy to light energy. Some energy is always wasted when energy changes form. When the light bulb produces light, it also produces unwanted heat.

Kinetic Energy

Objects in motion have **kinetic energy.** Kinetic energy depends on speed and mass. If an object moves faster, it will have more kinetic energy. Picture a carpenter slowly swinging a hammer to hit a nail. There is not much kinetic energy. The nail will not move much. There is more kinetic energy if the carpenter swings the hammer faster. The nail will move more each time the hammer hits it.

Moving faster increases the kinetic energy of the skier.

An object with more mass has more kinetic energy. A rolling beach ball might have enough energy to knock down one wall of a sand castle. What if you rolled a basketball, which has more mass, at the same speed as the beach ball? The whole sand castle might be flattened, since the basketball has more kinetic energy.

Kinetic energy can change into other forms of energy. A windmill can change it into electric energy. A drumstick's kinetic energy becomes sound energy when it hits a drum. Kinetic energy can also become thermal energy. Your hands get warmer when you rub them together. The friction of your moving hands changes kinetic energy into thermal energy.

The dog and the flying disk are moving at the same speed. But the dog has more kinetic energy because it has more mass than the flying disk has.

Potential Energy

Potential energy is energy that does not cause any changes now but could cause changes in the future. There are different types of potential energy.

Potential energy due to gravity is one type. If a metal ball hangs from a string, it does not cause any change. But if it falls from the string, it will cause a change. It will dent the surface below it. The higher or heavier the ball is, the more potential energy it has.

A toy car that sits at the very top of a track also has potential energy. As the car moves down the track, the amount of potential energy decreases. It changes to kinetic energy because the car is in motion.

The hanging metal ball has potential energy due to gravity. The higher or heavier the ball is, the more potential energy it has.

When the metal ball falls, it changes the shape of the clay below it.

Another kind of potential energy is in a stretched rubber band or a compressed spring. The more a rubber band is stretched or a spring is compressed, the more potential energy each has.

Magnets have another kind of potential energy. When you bring the north poles of two magnets close together and release them, they automatically move apart. The potential energy of the magnets changes to kinetic energy.

In a similar way, two atoms have potential energy when they are brought close together. There are negative electrons on the outside of each atom. This causes the atoms to repel each other.

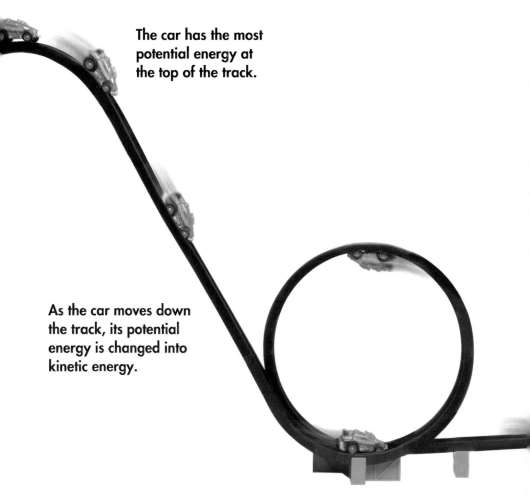

The car has the most potential energy at the top of the track.

As the car moves down the track, its potential energy is changed into kinetic energy.

Chemical Energy

Did you know that a match also has potential energy? It is in the form of chemical energy. This energy comes from the bonds between the atoms in molecules. Atoms bond when they share electrons or when electrons are transferred from one atom to another. Bonds with more electrons have more energy.

When fuel is burned in a car, furnace, or power plant, chemical energy is changed to heat and light energy. Different fuels have different kinds of molecules. Some molecules release more energy than others. Fuel for your body comes from food. Some foods give your body more energy than others. This energy is measured in units called kilocalories. When you discuss the number of calories in food, you are really talking about kilocalories.

When the fuel in the boat's engine burns, chemical energy is changed to kinetic, sound, and heat.

Nuclear Energy

Potential energy is also found within atoms. All atoms have tiny particles called protons, neutrons, and electrons. The nucleus is in the center of the atom. It contains the protons and neutrons. Electrons are outside of the nucleus.

A large amount of potential energy is found in the nucleus. Since all protons have the same charge, they push away from each other. But a very strong force called nuclear energy holds them together. Scientists have learned how to knock the protons apart. When this happens, the nuclear energy holding the protons together is released.

In a nuclear power plant, nuclear energy heats water. The water changes into steam. The steam is then used to make electrical energy.

What is sound energy?

What is sound?

Sound is produced when objects vibrate. A vibration is a quick back-and-forth movement. The vibrations are called waves. When waves travel through a material, the molecules of the material vibrate in a wave pattern. They get closer together and then move farther apart. The molecules bump into other particles. These particles move in a similar way, causing the wave to travel.

Areas where particles are close together are called crests. A wave's frequency is the number of crests that pass a certain point within a second. Frequency also measures how fast particles are vibrating. The greater the frequency is, the higher the pitch of the sound.

The harder you pluck the strings, the more kinetic energy changes into sound energy. The sound becomes louder.

Some sounds are louder than others. The source of the louder sounds vibrates more. Their sound waves have more energy. The energy squeezes the particles at the crests together. Loudness is measured in decibels (dB). If the loudness of a sound increases by ten dB, the sound has ten times more energy. If you often hear sounds that are louder than 90 dB, you may slowly lose your hearing. Sounds louder than 100 dB can damage your hearing very quickly.

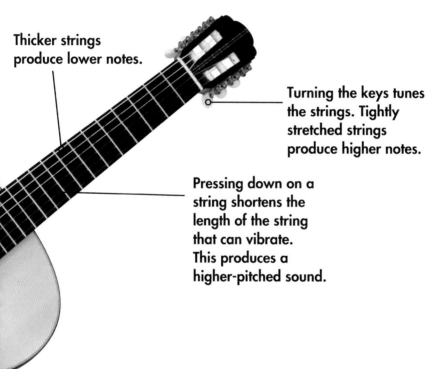

Thicker strings produce lower notes.

Turning the keys tunes the strings. Tightly stretched strings produce higher notes.

Pressing down on a string shortens the length of the string that can vibrate. This produces a higher-pitched sound.

Your Voice

When you talk, air rushes past your vocal cords. This causes them to vibrate. Then the vibrations move from your mouth to the air and travel as sound waves. These waves travel in all directions, so someone behind you can still hear what you are saying.

How does sound behave?

Sound waves travel through solids, liquids, and gases. But they cannot travel in a vacuum. A vacuum is an empty space with no particles. Sounds cannot be present without vibrating particles. Three different things can happen when sound waves reach a border between different materials. They can bounce back, be absorbed, or pass through.

Sound waves carry energy. This glass was broken by sound waves carrying a large amount of energy.

Sound travels at different speeds in different materials. Sound travels at about 1,500 meters per second in the ocean. The speed of sound may also change if the conditions of the material change. For example, the speed of sound in air depends on the air temperature. It travels at about 330 meters per second in 0°C air.

Sound waves can bounce off a surface such as a wall or cliff. The reflected sound is called an echo. The best way to hear your own echo is to face a wall and have your sound waves hit the wall at a 90° angle.

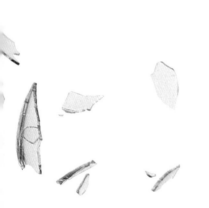

Material	Speed of Sound $(\frac{m}{s})$
dry air at sea level	331
iron	3,240
gold	1,200
glass	2,840
cork	500
maple wood	4,110
freshwater	1,498
saltwater	1,531

This chart shows the speed of sound through different materials. The speed of sound can also change if the conditions of the material change.

Sound Transfers Energy

In the picture below, the music studio's walls are lined with special soundproofing materials. Sound bounces around many times inside this material. Each time the sound bounces, the material vibrates. Some of the energy is turned into thermal energy. The material absorbs almost all the sound waves. This causes the sound to be muffled. Energy is changed from the kinetic energy of the piano keys to sound waves. The sound waves become thermal energy in the walls.

Music studios use soundproofing materials to eliminate echoes.

For sounds to be heard, an object must vibrate. Energy causes the vibrations. The vibrations give off energy as sound waves in air. When sound waves move, energy is transferred through the air. Some of the energy will reach your ears. Your eardrum will absorb some of this energy and begin to vibrate. This is how sound reaches you.

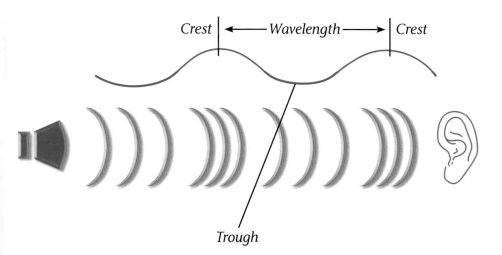

The sound you hear is a form of energy transferred by waves of vibration.

What is light energy?

Electromagnetic Radiation

Both light and sound are forms of energy that travel in waves. But unlike sound, light is not a vibration of particles. Light is a form of energy that is called **electromagnetic radiation.** This energy is both electrical and magnetic. The electrons in an object can give off light energy.

The electromagnetic radiation range has waves of many different frequencies and wavelengths. Visible light is only a small part of the full range. An object must reflect visible light for you to see it. The different colors that you see are different wavelengths.

Most electromagnetic waves cannot be seen. Some are shorter than those of visible light. Examples include ultraviolet, X-ray, and gamma radiation. These waves have higher frequencies and more energy than visible light.

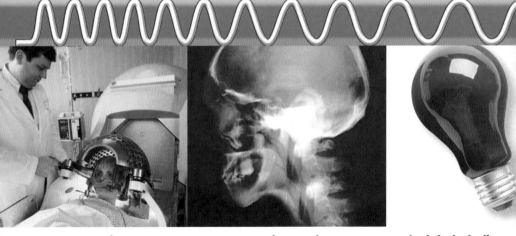

Gamma radiation can be used to kill cancer cells.

X rays can be used to see our bones.

Black light bulbs give off ultraviolet light.

Other forms of electromagnetic radiation have longer waves than visible light. Examples are infrared waves, microwaves, and radio waves. They have lower frequencies and lower energies than visible light. Most sources that give off visible light also give off heat. The heat is in the form of infrared waves.

Stars, such as the Sun, give off the most light in the universe. However, stars also give off different types of radiation, such as radio waves. The Sun transmits ultraviolet, infrared, X-ray, and other types of radiation.

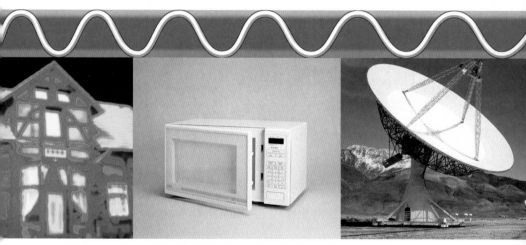

This infrared photograph shows that some parts of the house are hotter than others.

Microwave radiation is used to cook and heat up food.

Radio waves are used to send and receive signals for radio, television, and astronomy.

How does light move?

Electromagnetic waves are not vibrations of particles. Unlike sound waves, they can travel in a vacuum. Light travels in a vacuum at about 300 million meters per second. Light travels more slowly through materials such as air or water.

Usually light travels in straight lines. If the light reflects off an object such as a mirror, it still moves in a straight line. It just changes direction.

A submarine periscope has mirrors that reflect light from the surface. Then the sailor can see what's going on.

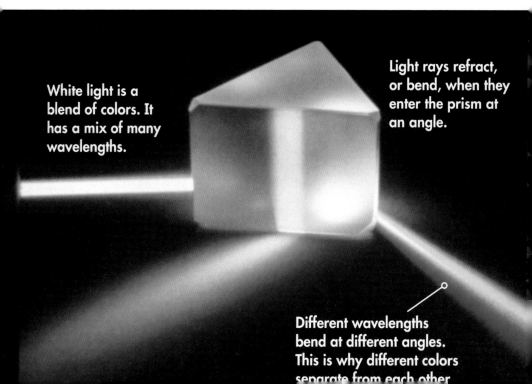

White light is a blend of colors. It has a mix of many wavelengths.

Light rays refract, or bend, when they enter the prism at an angle.

Different wavelengths bend at different angles. This is why different colors separate from each other

When light moves into a new material, it bends, or refracts. An example is when light enters a prism. A prism bends light of different wavelengths differently. White light that enters a prism becomes separated into its colors.

An object blocking the path of light waves causes shadows. Shadows are bigger when the object is bigger. They are also bigger when the object is closer to the light source.

Colored objects absorb some frequencies and wavelengths of light and reflect others. When light is absorbed, the energy is changed into thermal energy. The frequencies that are not absorbed are reflected. The colors we see depend on what frequencies are reflected by the object.

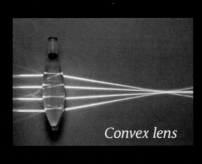

Convex lens

When light passes through a convex lens, the rays bend and come together at one point. Concave lenses cause light to spread out.

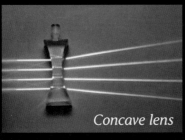

Concave lens

What is thermal energy?

When Matter Gets Warmer

A warm baked potato has a form of kinetic energy inside it. The atoms that make up the potato are always moving. Each atom has a certain amount of kinetic energy. **Thermal energy** is the total kinetic energy and potential energy of all the atoms in an object. When matter gets warmer, the kinetic energy of the atoms or molecules increases and the thermal energy increases.

Thermal Energy and Phase Changes

Matter can be a solid, a liquid, or a gas. A thermal energy change can cause a phase change. When thermal energy increases, a material's particles move faster. If the energy of a solid increases enough, it will melt into a liquid. The liquid state has more thermal energy than the solid state. If the liquid gains even more thermal energy, it can become a gas.

This beaker has liquid water, ice, and a balloon filled with air. All the materials have a temperature of 0°C.

Thermal Energy and Temperature

We measure thermal energy by measuring temperature. The temperature of an object describes the average kinetic energy of all its particles. When the particles move faster, the object will be warmer.

We use thermometers to measure temperature. The most common one uses a liquid inside a closed tube. When the temperature increases, the liquid expands. The height of the liquid rises or falls to show the temperature.

Thermal energy is added to the beaker when a flame is placed under it. As a result, the temperature rises, the ice melts, and the air in the balloon expands.

Conduction, Convection, Radiation

Thermal energy flows between materials of different temperatures. It flows from warmer to cooler materials. *Heat* is the word used to describe the flow of thermal energy.

Heat can move in three ways. **Conduction** occurs when heat flows between objects that are touching. **Convection** is when warm liquids or gases move to cooler areas. Radiation is energy moving as electromagnetic waves.

In conduction, two objects touch. Then their atoms or molecules collide. The faster-moving particles in the warmer object transfer some of their kinetic energy to the cooler object. When heat flows out, the warmer object decreases in temperature. The cooler object's temperature rises as heat flows into it. The heat flow goes on until both objects have the same temperature. If the two objects are made of the same material and have the same mass, then the temperature of one goes down by the same amount that the temperature of the other goes up.

Conduction

Conduction is the transfer of heat between two objects that are touching. In the picture on the right, the stove heats the pan by conduction. Conduction can also occur between different parts of the same object. The part of the handle closest to the stove will also heat up. As the heat continues to be transferred, the whole handle can become too hot to touch.

Convection

Convection is the transfer of heat by a moving liquid or gas. Cool water sinks below warmer water, and warm water rises. This movement, called a convection current, helps to heat this fish tank.

Radiation

Radiation is the transfer of heat by electromagnetic waves. All objects radiate heat. Hot objects radiate more heat than cool objects. In the picture, radiation from the Sun is used to warm the greenhouse.

Glossary

conduction the transfer of heat between objects that are touching

convection the transfer of heat by a moving liquid or gas

electromagnetic radiation a type of wave that is a combination of electric and magnetic energy

energy the ability to do work or cause a change

kinetic energy energy due to motion

potential energy energy that does not cause any changes now but could cause changes in the future

thermal energy the total kinetic and potential energy of all atoms in an object